ADLAR
POCK   K

G000292570

Boat name

Phonetic spelling

Call sign

Phonetic spelling

Length overall

Beam

Draft

Sail number

Height of mast

Water capacity

Fuel capacity

Skipper

Mobile

Email

Waypoint log

Waypoint No	Place	Latitude	Longitude

Waypoint No	Place	Latitude	Longitude

Waypoint log

Waypoint No	Place	Latitude	Longitude

Waypoint No	Place	Latitude	Longitude

Daily cruising log of yacht   *Merikala II*

Date	7th August 2007		
Port	Portsmouth	Port	Beaulieu
HW	05:20 HW 17.59	HW	05:47 HW 18:26
LW	10:46 LW 23:38	LW	11:13 LW 01:05

Time	Course	Log	Dist	Wind Dir	Force	Sea state
0800		0	–	S	1	Calm
0900	250	4.0	4.0	S	3	Calm
1000	270	6.5	2.5	S	2	Calm
1100	290	13.0	6.5	S	1	Calm

Notes and remarks

From	Portsmouth	Towards	Beaulieu
Crew	David, John		
Hours underway	5	Engine hours	1
Fuel consumption	2 litres	Fuel left	17 litres

Time	Notes
0630	Let go mooring
0800	Bacon butties
0900	Mid fort. Set main
1000	Good visibility. Passed Oasis
1100	Started engine, wind slack

Daily cruising log of yacht

Date						
Port			Port			
HW	HW		HW	HW		
LW	LW		LW	LW		

Time	Course	Log	Dist	Wind Dir	Force	Sea state

Notes and remarks

From		Towards	
Crew			
Hours underway		Engine hours	
Fuel consumption		Fuel left	

Time	Notes

Daily cruising log of yacht

Date						
Port			Port			
HW	HW		HW	HW		
LW	LW		LW	LW		

Time	Course	Log	Dist	Wind Dir	Force	Sea state

Notes and remarks

From	Towards
Crew	
Hours underway	Engine hours
Fuel consumption	Fuel left

Time	Notes

Daily cruising log of yacht

Date						
Port			Port			
HW	HW		HW	HW		
LW	LW		LW	LW		

Time	Course	Log	Dist	Wind Dir	Force	Sea state

Notes and remarks

From		Towards	
Crew			
Hours underway		Engine hours	
Fuel consumption		Fuel left	

Time	Notes

Daily cruising log of yacht

Date						
Port			Port			
HW	HW		HW	HW		
LW	LW		LW	LW		

Time	Course	Log	Dist	Wind Dir	Force	Sea state

Notes and remarks

From	Towards
Crew	
Hours underway	Engine hours
Fuel consumption	Fuel left

Time	Notes

Daily cruising log of yacht

Date

Port   Port

HW   HW   HW   HW

LW   LW   LW   LW

Time	Course	Log	Dist	Wind Dir	Force	Sea state

Notes and remarks

From	Towards
Crew	
Hours underway	Engine hours
Fuel consumption	Fuel left

Time	Notes

Daily cruising log of yacht

Date						
Port		Port				
HW	HW	HW	HW			
LW	LW	LW	LW			

Time	Course	Log	Dist	Wind Dir	Force	Sea state

Notes and remarks

From		Towards	
Crew			
Hours underway		Engine hours	
Fuel consumption		Fuel left	

Time	Notes

Daily cruising log of yacht

Date						
Port			Port			
HW	HW		HW	HW		
LW	LW		LW	LW		

Time	Course	Log	Dist	Wind Dir	Force	Sea state

Notes and remarks

From	Towards
Crew	
Hours underway	Engine hours
Fuel consumption	Fuel left

Time	Notes

Daily cruising log of yacht

Date						
Port			Port			
HW	HW		HW	HW		
LW	LW		LW	LW		

Time	Course	Log	Dist	Wind Dir	Force	Sea state

Notes and remarks

From	Towards
Crew	
Hours underway	Engine hours
Fuel consumption	Fuel left

Time	Notes

Daily cruising log of yacht

Date						
Port			Port			
HW	HW		HW	HW		
LW	LW		LW	LW		

Time	Course	Log	Dist	Wind Dir	Force	Sea state

Notes and remarks

From	Towards
Crew	
Hours underway	Engine hours
Fuel consumption	Fuel left

Time	Notes

Daily cruising log of yacht

Date						
Port			Port			
HW	HW		HW	HW		
LW	LW		LW	LW		

Time	Course	Log	Dist	Wind Dir	Force	Sea state

Notes and remarks

From	Towards
Crew	
Hours underway	Engine hours
Fuel consumption	Fuel left

Time	Notes

Daily cruising log of yacht

Date						
Port			Port			
HW HW			HW HW			
LW LW			LW LW			

Time	Course	Log	Dist	Wind Dir	Force	Sea state

Notes and remarks

From	Towards
Crew	
Hours underway	Engine hours
Fuel consumption	Fuel left

Time	Notes

Daily cruising log of yacht

Date						
Port			Port			
HW	HW		HW	HW		
LW	LW		LW	LW		

Time	Course	Log	Dist	Wind Dir	Force	Sea state

Notes and remarks

From	Towards
Crew	
Hours underway	Engine hours
Fuel consumption	Fuel left

Time	Notes

Daily cruising log of yacht

Date						
Port			Port			
HW	HW		HW	HW		
LW	LW		LW	LW		

Time	Course	Log	Dist	Wind Dir	Force	Sea state

Notes and remarks

From	Towards
Crew	
Hours underway	Engine hours
Fuel consumption	Fuel left

Time	Notes

Daily cruising log of yacht

Date						
Port			Port			
HW	HW		HW	HW		
LW	LW		LW	LW		

Time	Course	Log	Dist	Wind Dir	Force	Sea state

Notes and remarks

From	Towards
Crew	
Hours underway	Engine hours
Fuel consumption	Fuel left

Time	Notes

Daily cruising log of yacht

Date						
Port			Port			
HW	HW		HW	HW		
LW	LW		LW	LW		

Time	Course	Log	Dist	Wind Dir	Force	Sea state

Notes and remarks

From	Towards
Crew	
Hours underway	Engine hours
Fuel consumption	Fuel left

Time	Notes

Daily cruising log of yacht

Date						
Port			Port			
HW	HW		HW	HW		
LW	LW		LW	LW		

Time	Course	Log	Dist	Wind Dir	Force	Sea state

Notes and remarks

From	Towards
Crew	
Hours underway	Engine hours
Fuel consumption	Fuel left

Time	Notes

Daily cruising log of yacht

Date						
Port			Port			
HW	HW		HW	HW		
LW	LW		LW	LW		

Time	Course	Log	Dist	Wind Dir	Force	Sea state

Notes and remarks

From	Towards
Crew	
Hours underway	Engine hours
Fuel consumption	Fuel left

Time	Notes

Daily cruising log of yacht

Date						
Port			Port			
HW	HW		HW	HW		
LW	LW		LW	LW		

Time	Course	Log	Dist	Wind Dir	Force	Sea state

Notes and remarks

From	Towards
Crew	
Hours underway	Engine hours
Fuel consumption	Fuel left

Time	Notes

Daily cruising log of yacht

Date						
Port			Port			
HW	HW		HW	HW		
LW	LW		LW	LW		

Time	Course	Log	Dist	Wind Dir	Force	Sea state

Notes and remarks

From	Towards
Crew	
Hours underway	Engine hours
Fuel consumption	Fuel left

Time	Notes

Daily cruising log of yacht

Date						
Port			Port			
HW	HW		HW	HW		
LW	LW		LW	LW		

Time	Course	Log	Dist	Wind Dir	Force	Sea state

Notes and remarks

From		Towards	
Crew			
Hours underway		Engine hours	
Fuel consumption		Fuel left	

Time	Notes

Daily cruising log of yacht

Date						
Port			Port			
HW	HW		HW	HW		
LW	LW		LW	LW		

Time	Course	Log	Dist	Wind Dir	Force	Sea state

Notes and remarks

From	Towards
Crew	
Hours underway	Engine hours
Fuel consumption	Fuel left

Time	Notes

Daily cruising log of yacht

Date						
Port			Port			
HW	HW		HW	HW		
LW	LW		LW	LW		

Time	Course	Log	Dist	Wind Dir	Force	Sea state

Notes and remarks

From	Towards
Crew	
Hours underway	Engine hours
Fuel consumption	Fuel left

Time	Notes

Daily cruising log of yacht

Date

Port   Port

HW   HW   HW   HW

LW   LW   LW   LW

Time	Course	Log	Dist	Wind Dir	Force	Sea state

Notes and remarks

From	Towards
Crew	
Hours underway	Engine hours
Fuel consumption	Fuel left

Time	Notes

Daily cruising log of yacht

Date						
Port			Port			
HW	HW		HW	HW		
LW	LW		LW	LW		

Time	Course	Log	Dist	Wind Dir	Force	Sea state

Notes and remarks

From	Towards
Crew	
Hours underway	Engine hours
Fuel consumption	Fuel left

Time	Notes

Daily cruising log of yacht

Date						
Port			Port			
HW	HW		HW	HW		
LW	LW		LW	LW		

Time	Course	Log	Dist	Wind Dir	Force	Sea state

Notes and remarks

From		Towards	
Crew			
Hours underway		Engine hours	
Fuel consumption		Fuel left	

Time	Notes

Daily cruising log of yacht

Date						
Port			Port			
HW	HW		HW	HW		
LW	LW		LW	LW		

Time	Course	Log	Dist	Wind Dir	Force	Sea state

Notes and remarks

From	Towards
Crew	
Hours underway	Engine hours
Fuel consumption	Fuel left

Time	Notes

Daily cruising log of yacht

Date						
Port			Port			
HW	HW		HW		HW	
LW	LW		LW		LW	

Time	Course	Log	Dist	Wind Dir	Force	Sea state

Notes and remarks

From	Towards
Crew	
Hours underway	Engine hours
Fuel consumption	Fuel left

Time	Notes

Daily cruising log of yacht

Date						
Port			Port			
HW	HW		HW	HW		
LW	LW		LW	LW		

Time	Course	Log	Dist	Wind Dir	Force	Sea state

Notes and remarks

From	Towards
Crew	
Hours underway	Engine hours
Fuel consumption	Fuel left

Time	Notes

Daily cruising log of yacht

Date						
Port			Port			
HW	HW		HW	HW		
LW	LW		LW	LW		

Time	Course	Log	Dist	Wind Dir	Force	Sea state

Notes and remarks

From	Towards
Crew	
Hours underway	Engine hours
Fuel consumption	Fuel left

Time	Notes

Daily cruising log of yacht

Date						
Port			Port			
HW	HW		HW	HW		
LW	LW		LW	LW		

Time	Course	Log	Dist	Wind Dir	Force	Sea state

Notes and remarks

From	Towards
Crew	
Hours underway	Engine hours
Fuel consumption	Fuel left

Time	Notes

Daily cruising log of yacht

Date						
Port			Port			
HW	HW		HW	HW		
LW	LW		LW	LW		

Time	Course	Log	Dist	Wind Dir	Force	Sea state

Notes and remarks

From	Towards
Crew	
Hours underway	Engine hours
Fuel consumption	Fuel left

Time	Notes

Daily cruising log of yacht

Date						
Port			Port			
HW	HW		HW	HW		
LW	LW		LW	LW		

Time	Course	Log	Dist	Wind Dir	Force	Sea state

Notes and remarks

From	Towards
Crew	
Hours underway	Engine hours
Fuel consumption	Fuel left

Time	Notes

Daily cruising log of yacht

Date						
Port			Port			
HW	HW		HW	HW		
LW	LW		LW	LW		

Time	Course	Log	Dist	Wind Dir	Force	Sea state

Notes and remarks

From		Towards	
Crew			
Hours underway		Engine hours	
Fuel consumption		Fuel left	

Time	Notes

Daily cruising log of yacht

Date						
Port			Port			
HW	HW		HW		HW	
LW	LW		LW		LW	

Time	Course	Log	Dist	Wind Dir	Force	Sea state

Notes and remarks

From	Towards
Crew	
Hours underway	Engine hours
Fuel consumption	Fuel left

Time	Notes

Daily cruising log of yacht

Date						
Port			Port			
HW	HW		HW		HW	
LW	LW		LW		LW	

Time	Course	Log	Dist	Wind Dir	Force	Sea state

Notes and remarks

From	Towards
Crew	
Hours underway	Engine hours
Fuel consumption	Fuel left

Time	Notes

Daily cruising log of yacht

Date						
Port		Port				
HW	HW	HW	HW			
LW	LW	LW	LW			

Time	Course	Log	Dist	Wind Dir	Force	Sea state

Notes and remarks

From	Towards
Crew	
Hours underway	Engine hours
Fuel consumption	Fuel left

Time	Notes

Daily cruising log of yacht

Date						
Port			Port			
HW	HW		HW	HW		
LW	LW		LW	LW		

Time	Course	Log	Dist	Wind Dir	Force	Sea state

Notes and remarks

From		Towards	
Crew			
Hours underway		Engine hours	
Fuel consumption		Fuel left	

Time	Notes

Daily cruising log of yacht

Date

Port   Port

HW   HW   HW   HW
LW   LW   LW   LW

Time	Course	Log	Dist	Wind Dir	Force	Sea state

Notes and remarks

From	Towards
Crew	
Hours underway	Engine hours
Fuel consumption	Fuel left

Time	Notes

Daily cruising log of yacht

Date						
Port		Port				
HW	HW	HW	HW			
LW	LW	LW	LW			

Time	Course	Log	Dist	Wind Dir	Force	Sea state

Notes and remarks

From	Towards
Crew	
Hours underway	Engine hours
Fuel consumption	Fuel left

Time	Notes

Daily cruising log of yacht

Date						
Port		Port				
HW	HW	HW	HW			
LW	LW	LW	LW			

Time	Course	Log	Dist	Wind Dir	Force	Sea state

Notes and remarks

From	Towards
Crew	
Hours underway	Engine hours
Fuel consumption	Fuel left

Time	Notes

Daily cruising log of yacht

Date						
Port			Port			
HW	HW		HW	HW		
LW	LW		LW	LW		

Time	Course	Log	Dist	Wind Dir	Force	Sea state

Notes and remarks

From		Towards	
Crew			
Hours underway		Engine hours	
Fuel consumption		Fuel left	

Time	Notes

Daily cruising log of yacht

Date						
Port			Port			
HW	HW		HW	HW		
LW	LW		LW	LW		

Time	Course	Log	Dist	Wind Dir	Force	Sea state

Notes and remarks

From	Towards
Crew	
Hours underway	Engine hours
Fuel consumption	Fuel left

Time	Notes

Guests and friends

Date	Name	Address

Post code	Telephone	Email

Routine checks

Date	Comments	Routine checks
		Fuel level
		Engine oil
		Oil filter
		Batteries
		Coolant
		Fan belt
		Impeller
		Seacocks
		Extinguishers
		Head
		Bilge
		Engine start
		Water level
		Gas
		On deck
		Standing rigging
		Windlass
		Anchors
		Running rigging
		Sails
		Steering
		Lines
		Lifebelt

Spare parts needed

Item	Part No	Source	Tel No

Published by Adlard Coles Nautical
an imprint of A & C Black Publishers Ltd
38 Soho Square, London W1D 3HB
www.adlardcoles.com

First edition 2008

ISBN 978-0-7136-8870-2

This book is produced using paper that is made from
wood grown in managed, sustainable forests. It is natural,
renewable and recyclable. The logging and manufacturing
processes conform to the environmental regulations of the
country of origin.

Design by Fred Barter – Bosun Publications

Typeset in 8pt Franklin Gothic
Printed and bound in China by WKT